Why Dogs Bark and How To Stop It: Strategies For Dealing With Excessive Barking

By

Sandra Shillington

© Copyright 2023 by Sandra Shillington

All rights reserved.

This document is geared towards providing reliable information with regard to the topic covered. It does not represent professional advice. It is not intended to provide specific guidance for particular circumstances, and it should not be relied upon as the basis for for any decision to take action or not take action on any matter which it covers. If advice is necessary, a practiced individual in the profession should be consulted where appropriate, before making any such decision.

In no way is it legal to reproduce, duplicate or transmit any part of this document in either its electronic means or in printed format. Recording of this publication is strictly prohibited and any storage of this document is not allowed unless written permission from the publisher. All rights reserved.

The information provided herein is stated to be truthful and consistent, in that any liability, in terms of inattention or otherwise, by any usage or abuse of any policies, processes, or directions contained within is the solitary and utter responsibility of the recipient reader. Under no circumstances will any legal responsibility or blame be held against the publisher for any reparation, damages, or monetary loss due to the information herein, either directly or indirectly

Introduction

Dogs are wonderful companions, known for their loyalty, affection, and communication abilities. One of the most common ways dogs express themselves is through barking. Barking is a natural behavior for dogs and serves various purposes, but when it becomes excessive, it can become a problem for both the dog and its owners.

The purpose of this guide is to delve into the reasons behind dogs' barking behavior and provide effective strategies to reduce excessive barking. By understanding the underlying causes of barking and implementing appropriate training and management techniques, dog owners can create a harmonious and peaceful environment for both themselves and their canine friends.

This guide will cover the reasons why dogs bark, the impact of excessive barking on dogs and their owners, and explore various training methods and tools that can be used to address this behavior.

Additionally, it will highlight breed-specific considerations and natural remedies that may help in managing barking. It will also discuss when professional help may be necessary to tackle more complex cases of excessive barking.

Chapter 1
Understanding Dog Psychology

Animal psychology, also known as comparative psychology or animal behavior, is the scientific study of the behavior, cognition, and emotions of animals, including both domestic and wild species. It aims to understand the similarities and differences in behavior between different animal species, including humans. While there are similarities between animal and human psychology, there are also significant distinctions:

Cognitive Differences

Human Psychology: Humans have highly developed cognitive abilities, including complex thinking, problem-solving, and abstract reasoning. Humans can engage in introspection and have a self-awareness that allows them to reflect on their thoughts and emotions.

Animal Psychology: Animals vary in their cognitive abilities, and while some species demonstrate problem-solving and memory skills, their cognitive processes are generally less complex than humans. Few animals show evidence of self-awareness, and their thoughts and emotions are more instinctual and reactive.

Communication

Human Psychology: Humans have a sophisticated system of communication, including verbal language, written language, and non-verbal cues like facial expressions and body language. This allows for complex social interactions and the expression of abstract ideas.

Animal Psychology: Animals communicate using various methods, including vocalizations, body language, and scent marking. While some animals have relatively complex communication systems, they are generally more limited compared to human language.

Culture

Human Psychology: Humans have a rich cultural heritage, and societies pass down knowledge, beliefs, and traditions through generations. Culture influences human behavior and shapes social norms and values.

Animal Psychology: While some animals exhibit learned behaviors within their social groups, they do not possess culture in the same way as humans. Their behavior is more instinctual and influenced by genetic and environmental factors.

Emotions and Empathy

Human Psychology: Humans experience a wide range of emotions, including happiness, sadness, fear, anger, and empathy. Humans can understand and respond to the emotions of others, displaying empathy and compassion.

Animal Psychology: Animals also experience emotions, such as joy, fear, and affection, although the range and complexity of their emotions may be less than humans. Some animals display empathy-like behaviors towards others, particularly within their social groups.

Dogs feel emotions, and there is evidence to suggest that they can display empathy towards humans and other animals. Emotions are a fundamental part of being a social animal, and dogs, as descendants of wolves, have evolved to experience a range of emotions similar to humans.

What Emotions Do Dogs Have?

Happiness: Dogs express happiness through wagging tails, relaxed body postures, and playfulness. They are known to feel joy and contentment when they are with their human companions or engaged in activities they enjoy.
Fear: Dogs can experience fear in response to perceived threats or stressful situations. Common signs of fear include cowering, trembling, panting, and seeking comfort from their owner.

Anxiety: Dogs can feel anxious, especially when they are separated from their owners or exposed to unfamiliar environments. Excessive barking, pacing, and destructive behavior are signs of anxiety.

Love and Affection: Dogs form strong emotional bonds with their human family members and can display love and affection through physical contact, such as licking, nuzzling, and leaning against their owners.

Grief and Loss: Dogs can experience grief and sadness when they lose a companion or a family member. They may show signs of mourning, such as loss of appetite or reduced interest in activities.

Empathy in Dogs

Empathy is the ability to understand and share the feelings of others, and there is growing evidence to suggest that dogs display empathetic behavior. Some studies have shown that dogs can recognize and respond to human emotions, such as comfort-seeking behaviors when their owners are sad or upset. They may also respond to distress in other animals or show concern when other dogs are anxious or in pain.

It's important to note that the emotional range and depth in dogs may not be exactly the same as in humans. Dogs' emotional experiences are influenced by their genetics, life experiences, and socialization. While they may not comprehend emotions in the same complex way as humans, their ability to feel emotions and demonstrate empathy is significant.

As dog owners, understanding and respecting our dogs' emotions and empathetic responses can strengthen the human-dog bond and contribute to a positive and loving relationship. Providing a safe and supportive environment for our canine companions allows them to experience a wide range of emotions and thrive as social and emotional beings.

How Dogs Show Emotion

Dogs display emotions through a combination of body language, vocalizations, and behavior. As social animals, they have evolved to communicate their feelings to other dogs and humans. Understanding physical cues can help you determine what is driving their behavior. Here are some common ways dogs display certain emotions:

Tail Wagging: A wagging tail is one of the most recognizable signs of a dog's emotions. It can indicate happiness, excitement, or friendliness. However, the speed and position of the tail can convey different emotions. A high and fast wag might indicate enthusiasm, while a low and slow wag could signal submission or uncertainty.

Body Posture: Dogs use their body posture to communicate various emotions. For example:

Raised hackles: Can indicate fear, arousal, or aggression.

Relaxed body: A loose and relaxed body posture generally suggests that the dog is calm and comfortable.

Cowering: A dog cowering or tucking its tail between its legs might be feeling fearful or submissive.

Facial Expressions: Dogs can display a range of facial expressions, including:

Happy face: Relaxed mouth, bright eyes, and raised ears can indicate a happy and content dog.

Alertness: When a dog's ears are pricked, and their eyes are wide, they might be feeling attentive or alert.

Stress or fear: A dog might show signs of stress or fear through yawning, lip licking, or averting their gaze.

Vocalizations: Dogs use various vocalizations to express their emotions:

Barking: Can indicate excitement, alertness, anxiety, or territorial behavior.

Howling: Often associated with loneliness, separation anxiety, or a response to sirens or other howling dogs.

Whining or whimpering: May signal discomfort, anxiety, or a desire for attention.

Physical Contact: Dogs display affection and bonding through physical contact with humans and other animals. Nuzzling, leaning against you, or cuddling are ways dogs show their emotions.

Playfulness: When a dog engages in play, such as bowing, running around, and play-bowing, it indicates happiness and a desire for social interaction.

Licking: Licking can be a sign of affection and is a way dogs show their emotions towards their human or animal companions.

Destructive Behavior: When dogs engage in destructive behaviors, such as chewing on furniture or shoes, it might indicate anxiety, boredom, or separation distress.

It's important to note that each dog is an individual, and their display of emotions can vary based on their personality and experiences. Understanding your dog's body language and behavior can help you better interpret their emotions and respond appropriately to their needs. Positive interactions, training, and a loving environment can foster a strong emotional bond with your canine companion.

Tool Use and Technology

Human Psychology: Humans are adept at using tools and developing technology to solve problems and improve their lives. Human societies have advanced technologically over time.

Animal Psychology: While some animals, such as primates and birds, use tools in their natural behaviors, their use is limited and less complex compared to human tool use.

Animal psychology and human psychology share some common elements, such as emotions, social behaviors, and problem-solving. However, human psychology is more complex and unique due to the advanced cognitive abilities, communication, culture, and technology that humans possess.

While it's natural for us to empathize with our beloved dogs, it's important to understand they don't think and feel exactly like we do. When it comes to dog training, understanding animal psychology is essential for gaining insights into the behaviors and cognitive processes of dogs. This helps us appreciate how they differ from humans so we can learn the best ways to approach behavioral issues.

Chapter 2
Understanding Your Dog's Bark

Let's delve into the fascinating world of canine communication, with a particular focus on understanding your dog's bark. Barking is an integral part of a dog's vocal repertoire, and deciphering its various nuances is crucial for building a stronger bond with our furry companions. By understanding the different types of barks and their potential meanings, we gain invaluable insights into our dogs' emotions, needs, and responses to the world around them. From the joyful bursts of excitement to the alerting calls of potential dangers, each bark serves as a unique expression of your dog's thoughts and feelings.

Why Do Dogs Bark?

Communication

Barking is a primary means of communication for dogs. They use different barks to convey various messages such as alerting their owners to potential threats, greeting or expressing excitement, and even indicating discomfort or pain.

Alerting and Warning

Dogs have a natural instinct to protect their territory and loved ones. Barking can be a way for them to warn against intruders or anything they perceive as a threat.

Expressing Emotions

Dogs are emotional creatures, and barking can be a way for them to express joy, fear, frustration, or loneliness.

Attention-Seeking

Barking can be a learned behavior to get attention from their owners. If a dog barks and is rewarded with attention, they may continue this behavior.

Boredom and Anxiety

Barking can be a symptom of boredom or anxiety in dogs. They may bark excessively when left alone for long periods or if they lack mental and physical stimulation.

How do you know if your dog is bored or anxious?

Dogs can exhibit various behaviors that may indicate they are bored or anxious. It's essential to observe your dog's overall behavior and look for specific signs that suggest boredom or anxiety. Here are some common indicators of boredom and anxiety in dogs:

Signs of Boredom:

Destructive Behavior: **Bored dogs may engage in destructive behaviors, such as chewing on furniture, shoes, or household items.**

Excessive Barking: **Dogs may bark excessively when they are bored and seeking attention or stimulation.**

Restlessness: **Bored dogs may appear restless and have difficulty settling down or staying still.**

Lack of Interest: A bored dog may show disinterest in toys, activities, or their surroundings.

Attention-Seeking Behaviors: Dogs may seek attention from their owners in various ways, such as pawing, nudging, or jumping.

Digging: Boredom can lead to digging behavior, particularly in outdoor spaces.

Escaping: Bored dogs may try to escape from their confinement area or yard to seek stimulation elsewhere.

Repetitive Behaviors: Dogs may engage in repetitive behaviors, such as chasing their tail or pacing.

Signs of Anxiety:

Excessive Panting: Panting can be a sign of anxiety, especially when it occurs in non-stressful situations.

Trembling or Shaking: Anxious dogs may tremble or shake, particularly during stressful events or situations.

Pacing: Dogs with anxiety may pace back and forth as a way to cope with their stress.

Excessive Drooling: Anxiety can cause dogs to drool more than usual, even when they are not hot or thirsty.

Loss of Appetite: Anxious dogs may experience a reduced appetite or show disinterest in food.

Avoidance Behavior: Dogs may try to avoid certain situations or people if they cause anxiety.

Hiding: Anxious dogs may seek hiding spots as a way to cope with their fear or stress.

Excessive Licking or Grooming: Dogs may excessively lick or groom themselves when they are anxious.

Keep in mind that individual dogs may display different behaviors, and some signs can overlap between boredom and anxiety. If you notice concerning behaviors in your dog, it's essential to consult with a veterinarian or a certified dog behaviorist to determine the underlying cause and develop an appropriate plan to address your dog's needs. Creating a stimulating and enriching environment, providing regular exercise, and engaging in positive reinforcement training can help prevent boredom and reduce anxiety in dogs.

Breed-Specific Reasons for Barking

Different dog breeds have been bred for various purposes, and some breeds are more prone to barking due to their genetic traits and historical roles. For this reason, certain dog breeds may be more prone to excessive barking due to their natural instincts, temperament, and history of breeding for specific purposes. However, it's important to remember that individual dogs within any breed can vary in their barking tendencies. Here are some examples of dog breeds that are known to be more vocal and possibly more prone to barking excessively:

Beagle: Beagles have a strong hunting instinct, and they are known to use their bark to communicate with their pack during hunts.

Miniature Schnauzer: These small, intelligent dogs are alert and tend to bark to alert their owners of any perceived threats or strangers.

Chihuahua: Chihuahuas are known for their big personalities, and they can be quite vocal when they are excited or anxious.

Dachshund: Dachshunds were originally bred for hunting small game, and they may bark when they sense something unfamiliar or when they are bored.

Yorkshire Terrier: Yorkies are tiny but mighty when it comes to barking. They can be quite vocal and protective of their owners.

Pomeranian: Pomeranians have a lot of energy and can be quite vocal when they want attention or when they perceive a threat.

Shetland Sheepdog: Shelties are highly intelligent and alert herding dogs, and they may bark to express excitement, protectiveness, or boredom.

Siberian Husky: Huskies are known for their vocal nature, often "talking" and howling in addition to barking.

German Shepherd: These intelligent and protective dogs may bark to alert their owners, express anxiety, or respond to various triggers.

Fox Terrier: Fox Terriers are energetic and alert dogs that may bark to express their enthusiasm or alert their owners to potential threats.

Basset Hound: Basset Hounds have a distinctive baying bark, and they may bark when they catch an interesting scent or feel the need to communicate with their owners.

West Highland White Terrier: Westies are confident and independent dogs that may bark to express their feelings or alert their owners.

It's important to note that excessive barking in any breed can often be attributed to factors such as improper training, lack of socialization, anxiety, boredom, or medical issues. Proper training, positive reinforcement, and addressing the root cause of barking are essential in managing and reducing excessive barking in dogs, regardless of their breed.

The Negative Impacts of Excessive Barking

Noise Pollution

Excessive barking can create noise pollution, leading to disturbances for neighbors and possibly even legal issues if not addressed.

Neighbor Relations

Persistent barking can strain neighbor relations and may lead to conflicts and complaints.

Stress and Anxiety

Uncontrolled barking can increase stress and anxiety levels in both dogs and their owners.

Behavioral Issues

Excessive barking can sometimes be a symptom of underlying behavioral issues, and if left unaddressed, it may worsen or lead to other problematic behaviors.

Chapter 3
Strategies for Excessive Barking

Dealing with excessive barking in dogs can be a challenging but essential aspect of responsible pet ownership. Excessive barking can be a nuisance to neighbors, lead to complaints, and cause stress for both you and your dog. Fortunately, there are effective strategies to address this behavior and promote a calmer and more harmonious environment.

From understanding the underlying reasons for the barking to implementing positive reinforcement techniques and providing appropriate mental and physical stimulation, a comprehensive approach can help curb excessive barking and foster a well-behaved and content canine companion. Let's explore the various strategies to tackle excessive barking, so you can address this common behavioral issue with empathy, patience, and success.

Positive Reinforcement

Positive reinforcement is a fundamental and highly effective training technique when dealing with dog barking. It involves rewarding desired behaviors with positive consequences, such as treats, praise, or affection, to encourage the repetition of those behaviors. When applied to excessive barking, positive reinforcement can be a powerful tool in shaping a dog's behavior and promoting a quieter and more harmonious environment. The importance of positive reinforcement in this context can be understood through the following key points:

Encourages Desired Behavior: Dogs, like all living beings, seek rewards and positive experiences. By rewarding them for quiet behavior and not barking excessively, we reinforce the idea that being calm and silent leads to pleasant outcomes. Over time, the dog associates not barking with positive experiences and is more likely to exhibit the desired behavior.

Strengthens the human-canine bond: Positive reinforcement fosters trust, respect, and a strong bond between the dog and its owner. Dogs are social animals that thrive on positive interactions with their human companions. When we use positive reinforcement for desired behaviors, we establish a positive and loving relationship based on mutual understanding.

Promotes a positive learning experience: Punishment-based methods, such as scolding or yelling at a barking dog, can create fear, anxiety, and stress. These negative experiences hinder the learning process and can potentially lead to further behavioral issues. On the other hand, positive reinforcement creates a positive learning environment, making the training process enjoyable and engaging for the dog.

Focuses on what we want, instead of what we don't want: Positive reinforcement shifts the focus from punishing unwanted behavior to encouraging and reinforcing desired behavior. Instead of constantly trying to stop a dog from barking, we direct our attention to rewarding the moments of quietness, which is more productive and empowering.

Builds confidence and self-control: When dogs are consistently rewarded for good behavior, they become more confident and develop self-control. This increased self-control can help them manage their emotions better, reducing impulsive barking reactions to various triggers.

Encourages calmness: Using positive reinforcement to reinforce calm behavior helps dogs learn to relax and stay composed in different situations. This is especially valuable when dealing with barking triggered by anxiety, fear, or excitement.

Teaches dogs to communicate effectively: Dogs bark to communicate with humans and other animals. By positively reinforcing instances when a dog communicates appropriately or stops barking on command, we can shape better communication skills and ensure that barking is used purposefully rather than excessively.

Creates a happier living environment: Excessive barking can strain relationships with neighbors and affect the overall harmony of a household. By employing positive reinforcement to address barking issues, we create a quieter and more peaceful living environment for everyone involved.

Long-lasting effects: Positive reinforcement builds lasting associations between behavior and rewards. Unlike punishment-based methods, which may only suppress behavior temporarily, positive reinforcement can result in long-term changes and sustainable improvements in a dog's behavior.

Aligns with modern training principles: Positive reinforcement is widely endorsed by professional dog trainers and behaviorists. It is based on scientific principles of learning and has been proven to be a humane and effective method for training dogs.

Positive reinforcement is a powerful and humane approach to address excessive barking in dogs. It creates a positive learning experience, strengthens the bond between the dog and its owner, and encourages desired behavior, ultimately leading to a happier and more well-behaved canine companion.

Socialization and Mental Stimulation

Socialization and mental stimulation are powerful tools that dog owners can utilize to reduce excessive barking. Both of these strategies address the underlying causes of barking, such as fear, anxiety, boredom, and a lack of confidence. By implementing socialization and providing mental stimulation, dog owners can nurture a well-rounded and well-adjusted dog, leading to a quieter and happier pet.

Socialization

Early Start: Begin socializing your dog at a young age, ideally during the critical socialization period (between 3 and 16 weeks of age). This period is when dogs are most receptive to new experiences and learning how to interact positively with various people, animals, and environments.

Gradual Exposure: Introduce your dog to different sights, sounds, smells, and experiences in a controlled and positive manner. Gradually expose your dog to new situations, people, dogs, and places, taking care not to overwhelm them.

Positive Reinforcement: Use positive reinforcement techniques to reward your dog for calm and appropriate behavior during socialization. Offer treats, praise, or affection when your dog responds positively to new situations.

Observe Body Language: Be attentive to your dog's body language during socialization. If your dog shows signs of fear or discomfort, take a step back and allow them to approach new situations at their own pace.

Enroll in Training Classes: Enroll your dog in puppy or basic obedience training classes where they can interact with other dogs and people in a controlled environment. This will help build their confidence and teach them appropriate behaviors.

Mental Stimulation

Interactive Toys and Puzzles: Provide your dog with interactive toys and puzzles that require problem-solving and mental engagement. These toys challenge their minds and help alleviate boredom, which can be a significant trigger for excessive barking.

Hide and Seek: Play games of hide and seek with your dog, hiding treats or toys around the house or yard. This engages their sense of smell and keeps them mentally stimulated.

Training and Tricks: Teach your dog new tricks and commands. Training sessions not only provide mental stimulation, but also strengthen the bond between you and your dog.

Scent Work: Engage your dog's sense of smell by doing scent work activities. You can hide treats or toys for them to find, or even participate in scent detection training.

Daily Walks and Outings: Regular walks and outings provide mental stimulation through exposure to new sights, smells, and sounds. Exploring different environments can help your dog become more confident and less reactive, leading to reduced barking.

Playdates and Social Interactions: Organize playdates with other friendly and well-behaved dogs. Social interactions can be mentally stimulating and help your dog learn appropriate play behaviors.

By combining socialization and mental stimulation, you address the root causes of excessive barking. Socialization helps your dog feel more comfortable and confident in various situations, reducing anxiety-driven barking. Mental stimulation keeps your dog engaged and prevents boredom, which is another common trigger for barking. These strategies not only lead to a quieter dog but also contribute to a happier and well-adjusted pet that can better navigate the world around them.

Exercise and Physical Activity

Exercise and physical activity are essential components of managing and reducing excessive barking in dogs. Regular exercise helps fulfill a dog's natural energy and physical needs, promoting a balanced and contented state of mind. Here's how dog owners can use exercise and physical activity effectively to address barking issues:

Daily Walks: Take your dog for daily walks, ideally at least twice a day. Walking provides physical exercise, mental stimulation, and a chance for your dog to explore their environment, which can reduce restlessness and boredom, leading to less barking.

Jogging/Running: For more active breeds, consider jogging or running with your dog. This higher intensity exercise can help burn off excess energy and keep your dog physically tired, resulting in a calmer demeanor.

Playtime: Engage in interactive play sessions with your dog using toys such as balls, frisbees, or tug-of-war ropes. Playing fetch or engaging in games that involve physical activity helps release pent-up energy and reduces barking tendencies.

Mental Stimulation Through Physical Activities

Agility Training: Set up an agility course or use agility equipment in your backyard or at a local dog park. Agility training challenges both the body and mind, providing a great outlet for energy and reducing boredom-related barking.

Treibball: Treibball is a herding-type activity that involves pushing large balls into a goal using their nose or paws. It's mentally and physically stimulating for dogs, especially those with herding instincts.

Swimming: If your dog enjoys water, swimming is an excellent low-impact exercise that works the entire body. Swimming can be particularly beneficial for dogs with joint issues.

Scheduled Playdates: Arrange playdates with other friendly and well-socialized dogs. Playtime with canine friends offers both physical exercise and social interaction, which can reduce anxiety-driven barking.

Canine Sports: Enroll your dog in activities like flyball, dock diving, or lure coursing, depending on their interests and abilities. These sports provide physical exertion and mental stimulation, which can help alleviate barking due to boredom or frustration.

Consider Hiring a Dog Walker:

If you have a busy schedule and find it challenging to provide your dog with enough exercise during the day, consider hiring a professional dog walker. They can take your dog for walks and provide companionship, reducing pent-up energy that may lead to excessive barking.

Observe Your Dog's Behavior

Pay attention to your dog's behavior after exercise. If they are calmer and more relaxed, you can likely attribute their previous barking to a lack of physical activity.

By incorporating regular exercise and physical activities into your dog's daily routine, you help address the root causes of excessive barking, such as boredom, anxiety, and excess energy. A tired and mentally stimulated dog is less likely to engage in nuisance barking and is more likely to be content and well-behaved, contributing to a more harmonious and peaceful living environment for both the dog and its owners.

Desensitization and Counter Conditioning

Desensitization and counter-conditioning are powerful behavior modification techniques that can help dog owners address and reduce excessive barking triggered by specific stimuli, such as strangers, other dogs, or loud noises. These techniques work by changing the dog's emotional response to the trigger, gradually decreasing their fear or excitement and replacing it with a positive or neutral association. Here's how dog owners can use desensitization and counter-conditioning to stop dog barking:

Identify Triggers: The first step is to identify the specific triggers that cause your dog to bark excessively. Common triggers include strangers approaching, other dogs, loud noises (e.g., thunderstorms, fireworks), or specific objects.

Create a Hierarchy of Triggers: Rank the identified triggers in terms of their intensity or how much they affect your dog's barking behavior. Start with the least intense trigger and gradually work up to the most intense one.

Set the Threshold: Determine the distance or intensity at which the trigger is still present but does not cause excessive barking. This is the threshold level, and you'll use it during the desensitization process.

Desensitization

Introduce the Trigger Below Threshold: During training sessions, expose your dog to the trigger from a distance or intensity level that does not provoke excessive barking or fear. This ensures that your dog remains calm and receptive to learning.

Positive Reinforcement: While the trigger is present but below the threshold, use positive reinforcement techniques such as treats, praise, or affection to reward your dog for remaining calm and relaxed. This reinforces the association between the trigger and positive experiences.

Gradually Increase Exposure: Over time, gradually decrease the distance or intensity of the trigger, exposing your dog to it in a controlled manner. Continue rewarding calm behavior and ensuring that your dog feels safe and comfortable throughout the process.

Take it Slow: Progress at your dog's pace. If your dog shows signs of stress or barking, move back to a distance or intensity level where they are comfortable and then proceed more slowly.

Counter-Conditioning

Create Positive Associations: While desensitization reduces the dog's sensitivity to the trigger, counter-conditioning aims to replace the negative emotional response with a positive one. When the trigger is present, offer your dog highly desirable rewards, such as high-value treats or favorite toys.

Immediate Rewards: Provide the rewards as soon as the trigger appears, so your dog starts associating the trigger with positive experiences. This helps shift their emotional response from fear or excitement to a positive or neutral one.

Consistency and Patience: Both desensitization and counter-conditioning require consistency and patience. Progress may be slow, and it's essential to avoid rushing or pushing your dog beyond their comfort zone.

Seek Professional Help: If you are unsure about implementing desensitization and counter-conditioning on your own or if your dog's barking issues are severe, consider consulting a professional dog trainer or behaviorist. They can provide guidance and tailor a training plan specific to your dog's needs.

By using desensitization and counter-conditioning techniques, dog owners can effectively reduce excessive barking triggered by specific stimuli. The goal is to help your dog develop a more positive and relaxed response to these triggers, leading to a calmer and happier canine companion.

Managing the Environment and Triggers

Managing a dog's environment is a crucial aspect of addressing and stopping excessive barking. By making strategic adjustments to the dog's surroundings, owners can reduce the triggers that prompt barking and create a more peaceful living environment. Here are some effective ways dog owners can manage their dog's environment to stop excessive barking

Limit Visual Triggers

Close curtains or blinds: If your dog is triggered by seeing people or other animals passing by outside, close curtains or blinds to block their view. This can help reduce barking at perceived intruders.

Control Auditory Triggers

Reduce external noises: If your dog reacts strongly to external sounds like construction noise or sirens, consider using white noise machines, calming music, or playing the television at a low volume to mask the sounds and create a more soothing environment.

Provide a Safe and Comfortable Space

Create a safe zone: Designate a quiet and comfortable space in your home where your dog can retreat to when they feel anxious or overwhelmed. This area can be equipped with their bed, toys, and water bowl to help them feel secure.

Consider Anti-Barking Devices

Anti-bark collars: Consider using anti-bark collars that emit a harmless citronella spray, emit an ultrasonic sound, or vibrate when the dog barks excessively. These devices can help interrupt the barking behavior and discourage barking at certain triggers.

Automatic bark deterrents: Automatic bark deterrent devices can be placed in areas where your dog spends time, and they emit a sound or spray when they detect barking, discouraging the behavior.

Manage Social Interactions

Controlled social introductions: When introducing your dog to new people or animals, do so in a controlled and positive manner. Avoid overwhelming situations that might lead to fear-based barking.

Avoid Reinforcing Barking

Refrain from yelling: Yelling at a barking dog can inadvertently reinforce the barking behavior or increase their anxiety. Instead, remain calm and use positive reinforcement techniques to reward quiet behavior.

Be Consistent with Training

Training and reinforcement: Continually work on training your dog to respond to commands like "quiet" or "enough" when they start barking. Reward them when they obey the command to reinforce the desired behavior.

Address Underlying Issues

If your dog's excessive barking is driven by anxiety, fear, or other behavioral issues, address these underlying problems with the help of a professional dog trainer or behaviorist.

Use Exercise and Mental Stimulation

Providing regular exercise and mental stimulation can help reduce boredom and anxiety, leading to less barking due to pent-up energy.

Seek Professional Guidance

If excessive barking persists despite your efforts, consider seeking guidance from a professional dog trainer or behaviorist who can assess the specific situation and provide personalized strategies to stop the barking.

By managing the dog's environment and implementing positive reinforcement training techniques, dog owners can effectively reduce excessive barking and create a more peaceful and harmonious home for both their dog and themselves.

Tools and Devices for Controlling Barking

Anti-Bark Collars

Anti-bark collars are devices designed to deter dogs from barking excessively by delivering aversive stimuli when the dog barks. While these collars can be effective in reducing barking, they also come with both pros and cons that need to be carefully considered:

Pros:

Effective Barking Deterrent: Anti-bark collars can be effective in reducing or stopping excessive barking in some dogs. The aversive stimuli, such as a citronella spray, ultrasonic sound, or vibration, act as a deterrent, conditioning the dog to associate barking with an unpleasant experience.

Can be Automatic and Convenient: Some anti-bark collars are automatic and respond to the dog's barking, making them convenient for dog owners who may not always be present to address the barking behavior.

No Need for Owner Intervention: Unlike traditional training methods that require consistent owner intervention, anti-bark collars can work even when the owner is not present, helping to deter barking when the dog is alone.

Useful for Specific Situations: Anti-bark collars can be beneficial in specific situations where barking needs to be curbed quickly, such as in neighborhoods with noise restrictions or during times when quiet is necessary.

Cons:

Potential for Negative Side Effects: Anti-bark collars deliver aversive stimuli that may cause fear, anxiety, or stress in some dogs. These negative emotions can lead to behavioral issues, increased barking, or even aggression.

Overlooks the Root Cause: Anti-bark collars do not address the underlying reasons for excessive barking, such as anxiety, fear, or boredom. If the root cause is not addressed, the barking may persist or manifest in other unwanted behaviors.

Risk of Overcorrection: Anti-bark collars can be triggered by non-problematic barking or vocalizations, leading to overcorrection and confusion in the dog. This can result in the dog becoming anxious or developing other behavior problems.

May Impact the Human-Dog Bond: Using aversive stimuli to deter barking can affect the dog's trust in the owner and the overall human-dog relationship. The dog may associate the discomfort with the owner, leading to a breakdown in communication and bonding.

Not Effective for All Dogs: Some dogs may become desensitized to the aversive stimuli over time, rendering the collar ineffective. Additionally, certain breeds or individual dogs may be less responsive to the collar's deterrent.

Possible Unintended Associations: The aversive stimuli delivered by the collar might inadvertently become associated with triggers or situations unrelated to barking, causing the dog to develop fear or anxiety around those stimuli.

Potential for Skin Irritation or Discomfort: Depending on the type of anti-bark collar used, there is a risk of skin irritation or discomfort for some dogs, particularly those with sensitive skin.

While anti-bark collars can be a quick fix to address excessive barking in some dogs, they also come with potential risks and side effects. It is essential to weigh the pros and cons carefully and consider alternative training methods that use positive reinforcement and address the underlying causes of barking. If considering an anti-bark collar, consulting with a professional dog trainer who uses force-free and humane training methods can provide valuable guidance and ensure the well-being of the dog.

Ultrasonic Devices

Ultrasonic devices are tools designed to stop dog barking by emitting high-frequency sound waves that are not audible to humans but are irritating to dogs. These devices are considered non-invasive and are often marketed as a humane alternative to more aversive methods. However, like any training tool, ultrasonic devices have their own set of pros and cons:

Pros:

Non-Invasive and Harmless: Ultrasonic devices do not cause physical harm to dogs. The high-frequency sound they emit is generally considered safe and non-invasive.

No Collar Required: Unlike anti-bark collars, ultrasonic devices do not require the dog to wear anything, which can be beneficial for dogs who may be uncomfortable wearing collars.

Automatic Operation: Some ultrasonic devices are automatic and activate only when the dog barks, making them convenient for owners who may not always be present to address the barking behavior.

Can be Used at a Distance: Ultrasonic devices can be used from a distance, allowing owners to control the barking even when they are not close to the dog.

Can be Used for Other Unwanted Behaviors: Ultrasonic devices are not limited to stopping barking and can be used to deter other unwanted behaviors, such as jumping or digging.

Cons:

Effectiveness Varies: The effectiveness of ultrasonic devices can vary from dog to dog. Some dogs may be less affected or become desensitized to the sound over time, rendering the device less effective.

Possible Unintended Associations: Dogs may associate the high-frequency sound with other unrelated stimuli or situations, potentially causing fear or anxiety.

Overlooks the Root Cause: Ultrasonic devices do not address the underlying reasons for barking, such as anxiety or boredom. Using the device may temporarily stop the barking, but if the root cause is not addressed, the barking may return or manifest in other unwanted behaviors.

May Cause Stress: While ultrasonic devices are designed to be irritating rather than painful, some dogs may still find the sound stressful or frightening, leading to increased anxiety.

Limited Range and Obstacles: The effectiveness of ultrasonic devices can be hindered by obstacles, walls, or distance. They may not work effectively in large outdoor spaces or if the dog is not within the device's range.

No Positive Reinforcement: Ultrasonic devices rely solely on aversive stimuli and do not provide positive reinforcement for desired behaviors. This lack of positive reinforcement can limit the dog's motivation to behave appropriately.

Ethical Considerations: Some dog owners and animal welfare advocates raise ethical concerns about using any aversive training methods, including ultrasonic devices. They argue that positive reinforcement-based training methods are more respectful and effective in fostering a strong human-dog bond.

While ultrasonic devices can be a quick and non-invasive method to deter dog barking, their effectiveness and ethical considerations should be carefully weighed. It is essential to consider alternative training methods that use positive reinforcement and address the underlying causes of barking. If considering the use of an ultrasonic device, consulting with a professional dog trainer who uses force-free and humane training methods can provide valuable guidance and ensure the well-being of the dog.

Citronella Collars

Citronella collars are a type of anti-bark collar designed to stop dog barking by delivering a burst of citronella spray whenever the dog barks. This spray emits a strong citrus scent that is unpleasant to dogs but harmless. Like any training tool, citronella collars have their own set of pros and cons.

Pros:

Non-Invasive and Humane: Citronella collars are considered non-invasive and humane since they do not cause physical harm to dogs. The citronella spray acts as an annoyance rather than a painful stimulus.

Safe and Non-Toxic: Citronella spray is derived from natural sources and is generally safe for dogs. The spray does not cause any long-term harm and dissipates quickly.

No Collateral Damage: Unlike some other aversive methods, citronella collars do not have any physical impact on the dog, so there is no risk of causing injury or discomfort.

Effective for Some Dogs: Citronella collars can be effective in reducing or stopping excessive barking in certain dogs. The spray creates a negative association with barking, discouraging the behavior.

No Need for Owner Intervention: Automatic citronella collars activate in response to the dog's barking, making them convenient for dog owners who may not always be present to address the barking behavior.

Useful for Specific Situations: Citronella collars can be beneficial in specific situations where barking needs to be curbed quickly, such as in neighborhoods with noise restrictions or during times when quiet is necessary.

Cons:

Effectiveness Varies: The effectiveness of citronella collars can vary from dog to dog. Some dogs may become desensitized to the citronella scent over time, rendering the collar less effective.

Overlooks the Root Cause: Citronella collars do not address the underlying reasons for barking, such as anxiety, fear, or boredom. If the root cause is not addressed, the barking may persist or manifest in other unwanted behaviors.

May Cause Stress or Fear: While citronella spray is not harmful, some dogs may find the scent stressful or frightening, leading to increased anxiety.

Possible Unintended Associations: Dogs may associate the citronella spray with other unrelated stimuli or situations, potentially causing fear or anxiety.

Maintenance and Refills: Citronella collars require regular maintenance, including refilling the citronella spray, which can be an ongoing cost.

Limited Range and Obstacles: The effectiveness of citronella collars can be hindered by obstacles, walls, or distance. They may not work effectively in large outdoor spaces or if the dog is not within the collar's range.

No Positive Reinforcement: Citronella collars rely solely on aversive stimuli and do not provide positive reinforcement for desired behaviors. This lack of positive reinforcement can limit the dog's motivation to behave appropriately.

Ethical Considerations: Some dog owners and animal welfare advocates raise ethical concerns about using any aversive training methods, including citronella collars. They argue that positive reinforcement-based training methods are more respectful and effective in fostering a strong human-dog bond.

Citronella collars can be a non-invasive method to deter dog barking, but their effectiveness and ethical considerations should be carefully weighed. It is essential to consider alternative training methods that use positive reinforcement and address the underlying causes of barking. If considering the use of a citronella collar, consulting with a professional dog trainer who uses force-free and humane training methods can provide valuable guidance and ensure the well-being of the dog.

Natural and Home Remedies for Barking

Herbal Supplements and Calming Aids

Herbal supplements and calming aids for dogs are products designed to help reduce stress, anxiety, and promote relaxation in dogs. They typically contain natural ingredients that are believed to have calming properties. Here are some pros and cons of using herbal supplements and calming aids for dogs.

Pros:

Natural Ingredients: Herbal supplements and calming aids are often made from natural ingredients, which can be appealing to dog owners who prefer a more holistic approach to managing their dog's stress and anxiety.

Non-Sedative Options: Many herbal supplements and calming aids do not contain sedatives or other strong medications, making them a gentler option for calming anxious dogs.

Promote Relaxation: When used appropriately, these supplements can help promote relaxation in dogs, making them useful for stressful situations such as thunderstorms, fireworks, car rides, or vet visits.

May Reduce Undesirable Behaviors: By reducing anxiety and stress, herbal supplements can help decrease undesirable behaviors associated with fear, such as excessive barking, destructive chewing, or urination indoors.

Available Over-the-Counter: In many cases, herbal supplements and calming aids can be purchased over-the-counter without a prescription, making them easily accessible to dog owners.

Cons:

Varied Efficacy: The effectiveness of herbal supplements and calming aids can vary from dog to dog. What works for one dog may not work for another, and some dogs may not respond to the supplements at all.

Lack of Scientific Evidence: While some individual herbs may have studies supporting their calming effects, the overall efficacy of many herbal supplements and calming aids lacks strong scientific evidence due to limited research.

Possible Allergic Reactions: Dogs can have allergic reactions to certain herbal ingredients, which may lead to adverse effects. It's essential to monitor your dog closely after starting any new supplement.

Underlying Health Issues: Herbal supplements may interact with other medications or underlying health conditions your dog has. It's crucial to consult with your veterinarian before adding any supplements to your dog's regimen.

Not a Substitute for Training: Herbal supplements and calming aids should not replace proper training and behavior modification for anxious dogs. Addressing the root cause of anxiety is essential for long-term improvement.

Unregulated Products: The supplement industry is not as strictly regulated as pharmaceuticals, which means some products may vary in quality and potency.

Placebo Effect: In some cases, the calming effects of herbal supplements may be attributed to the placebo effect, where the owner's belief in the product's efficacy influences their perception of the dog's behavior.

Herbal supplements and calming aids can be a useful addition to a comprehensive approach to managing a dog's stress and anxiety. While they may provide some relief and relaxation, they should be used in conjunction with behavior modification, training, and under the guidance of a veterinarian. Not every dog will benefit from these supplements, and it's essential to consider each dog's unique needs and consult with a professional before incorporating any new supplements into their routine.

White Noise and Music

Using white noise and music as a calming technique for anxious barking dogs can be effective in some cases. These auditory tools can help create a soothing environment and mask external noises that may trigger anxiety or excessive barking. Here's how they work and their effectiveness.

White Noise

White noise is a consistent, gentle sound that covers a wide range of frequencies, effectively masking other sounds in the environment. The continuous sound helps drown out sudden or jarring noises, which can be unsettling for dogs and contribute to their anxiety. By reducing the audibility of external triggers, white noise can create a more calming and predictable atmosphere for the dog.

Effectiveness of White Noise

White noise can be particularly effective in reducing anxiety caused by sudden or loud sounds, such as thunderstorms, fireworks, or construction noise. It can also be useful for dogs who experience separation anxiety, as it helps minimize external stimuli that may trigger distress when the owner is away. However, its effectiveness may vary depending on the dog's individual preferences and the severity of their anxiety.

Music

Music therapy for dogs involves playing calming, soothing, and classical music designed to relax and reduce stress. The music's tempo, rhythm, and melody can influence the dog's heart rate and stress levels, promoting a sense of calmness. Music with slow, steady beats and minimal vocalization tends to be most effective in creating a calming environment.

Effectiveness of Music

Studies have shown that playing calming music can reduce stress and anxiety in dogs. It can help lower heart rate and cortisol levels, which are indicators of stress. Music can also create a positive association with relaxation, making it beneficial during stressful events or when the dog is left alone. Music is particularly useful in multi-dog households, as it can have a calming effect on all the dogs in the environment.

Combining White Noise and Music

Combining white noise with calming music can enhance the overall calming effect for anxious barking dogs. White noise helps to mask external triggers, while calming music contributes to relaxation and reduces anxiety. The combined use of these auditory tools can create a more soothing and stress-free environment for the dog.

Important Considerations

It's essential to select appropriate white noise and music that are specifically designed for dogs. Regular white noise or music for humans may not have the desired calming effect.

The volume level should be adjusted to a comfortable level for the dog. Loud or sudden noises can have the opposite effect and increase anxiety.

Calming auditory tools should be used in conjunction with other behavior modification techniques and training to address the underlying causes of anxiety and excessive barking.

Using white noise and calming music can be an effective strategy to calm anxious barking dogs, especially during stressful events or when left alone. However, its effectiveness may vary depending on the individual dog's response and the severity of their anxiety. Incorporating these auditory tools into a comprehensive anxiety management plan can help create a more relaxed and peaceful environment for the dog.

Training with Treats and Toys

Using treats and toys can be an effective positive reinforcement strategy to stop a dog from barking. The key is to redirect their focus and reward them for being quiet. Here's how to use treats and toys to address excessive barking:

Identify the Trigger

Observe your dog to identify the specific triggers that cause them to bark excessively. Common triggers include strangers approaching, doorbells, other dogs, or loud noises.

Train the "Quiet" Command

Choose a quiet and calm environment to start the training.
Hold a treat or a favorite toy in your hand to get your dog's attention.

Wait for a moment of silence, even if brief, and say "Quiet" in a calm and firm voice.
Immediately reward your dog with the treat or toy and offer praise for being quiet.

Practice with Controlled Triggers
Introduce controlled triggers in a gradual manner. For example, have a friend ring the doorbell from a distance or play a recording of a sound that typically triggers barking.

As soon as your dog begins barking, use the "Quiet" command and wait for a moment of silence before rewarding them with treats or toys.

Stay Consistent
Consistency is essential in this training. Reward your dog each time they respond to the "Quiet" command and remain consistent in using the command when they bark at triggers.

Use High-Value Treats and Toys

Use treats or toys that your dog finds highly rewarding. High-value treats are especially useful in reinforcing desired behaviors effectively.

Gradually Increase Duration

As your dog becomes more familiar with the "Quiet" command, gradually increase the time they need to remain quiet before receiving the reward. This encourages them to stay quiet for longer periods.

Be Patient and Positive

Training takes time, and every dog learns at their own pace. Be patient and maintain a positive attitude throughout the process.

Avoid Punishment

Avoid punishing your dog for barking, as it can create fear or anxiety and worsen the barking behavior. Positive reinforcement is a more effective and humane approach.

Provide Mental Stimulation

Keep your dog mentally stimulated with interactive toys, puzzle games, and activities to prevent boredom, which can contribute to excessive barking.

Seek Professional Help if Needed
If your dog's barking issues are severe or if you're facing challenges in the training process, consider seeking help from a professional dog trainer or behaviorist. They can provide personalized guidance and support to address the specific issues your dog is experiencing.

Remember that positive reinforcement is a more effective and humane way to modify behavior, and using treats and toys can help create a positive association with being quiet, leading to a calmer and more well-behaved dog.

Dealing With Separation Anxiety

Dealing with separation anxiety in your dog requires patience, understanding, and a comprehensive approach. Here are some steps you can take to help your dog cope with separation anxiety:

Gradual Desensitization

Gradually acclimate your dog to being alone by leaving for short periods and gradually increasing the time away. This helps them build confidence and reduces anxiety about your departures.

Gradual desensitization is a highly effective technique to help ease separation anxiety in dogs. It involves exposing the dog to the trigger (being alone) in a controlled and gradual manner, allowing them to become more comfortable and less anxious over time. Here are the steps for implementing gradual desensitization to address separation anxiety:

- **Start with Short Absences:** Begin by leaving your dog alone for very short periods, such as just a few seconds to a minute. Stay within your dog's sight but avoid direct interaction. Gradually increase the time you are away in small increments.
- **Create a Safe Space:** Designate a specific area or room as your dog's safe space. Make it comfortable with their bed, toys, and familiar

scents. This area will serve as their "happy place" and help them feel secure during your absences.
- **Use a Cue:** Create a consistent cue or phrase that signals your departure, such as saying "be right back." Using the same cue each time helps your dog understand that you will return.
- **Stay Calm:** Before leaving and returning home, maintain a calm and low-key demeanor. Avoid excessive attention or long goodbyes, as they can increase your dog's anxiety.

Short Departures and Returns: During the desensitization process, make sure your departures and returns are brief and predictable. This helps your dog understand that your absences are temporary and that you will always come back.
- **Vary the Routine:** Mix up your departure routine so that your dog does not anticipate your actions and get anxious when they recognize the signs of your impending departure.
- **Extend Absences Gradually:** As your dog becomes more comfortable with short absences, gradually extend the time you are away. Increase the duration in small increments, making sure your dog remains relaxed and at ease during each step.

- **Monitor Your Dog's Response:** Pay close attention to your dog's behavior during the desensitization process. If they show signs of stress or anxiety, take a step back to a shorter absence duration where they are more comfortable.
- **Reward Calm Behavior:** When you return home and find your dog calm and relaxed, reward them with praise, treats, or affection. This positive reinforcement helps them associate your return with positive experiences.
- **Be Patient and Consistent:** Gradual desensitization takes time and consistency. It is essential to be patient with your dog's progress and celebrate even small improvements.

Remember the pace of desensitization may vary with each dog. Some dogs may progress quickly, while others may require more time and patience. If your dog's separation anxiety is severe or if you encounter challenges during the desensitization process, consider seeking guidance from a professional dog trainer or behaviorist to develop a tailored plan that best suits your dog's needs.

Use Interactive Toys

Provide your dog with interactive toys or puzzle feeders filled with treats to keep them mentally stimulated while you're away.

Leave a Piece of Clothing

Leave a piece of your clothing with your scent on it near your dog's sleeping area. Your scent can provide comfort and reassurance.

Background Noise

Leaving on soft background noise, such as a radio or TV, can help mask external sounds and create a more soothing environment.

Practice Absence Inside

Practice brief absences inside the house while your dog is in their safe space. This helps them understand that you will return.

Seek Professional Training

Consider consulting a professional dog trainer or behaviorist experienced in separation anxiety. They can provide personalized strategies and guidance.

Refer to Chapter 4 for tips on finding a dog training professional.

Counter-Conditioning

Use positive reinforcement techniques to change your dog's emotional response to your departure. For example, give treats or toys only when you leave, so they associate your departure with something positive.

Counter conditioning is a behavior modification technique used in dog training to change a dog's emotional response to a specific stimulus or situation. The goal of counter conditioning is to replace the dog's negative or undesirable reaction with a positive and more appropriate response. This technique is commonly employed to address fear, anxiety, or aggression-related behaviors in dogs.

The process of counter conditioning involves pairing the presence of the trigger (the stimulus that elicits the unwanted behavior) with something the dog enjoys or finds rewarding. The positive association with the trigger helps to change the dog's emotional response from fear, anxiety, or aggression to a more relaxed or positive state. Here's how counter conditioning works:

- **Identify the Trigger:** The first step is to identify the specific trigger that causes the dog's unwanted behavior. It could be anything from meeting new people to encountering other dogs or loud noises.
  Determine the Reward: Find out what rewards or treats the dog finds most enticing. It could be their favorite treat, a toy, or verbal praise.
  Distance and Threshold: Start at a distance where the dog can see or hear the trigger but does not display any negative behavior. This distance is known as the threshold distance, where the dog is still comfortable.
- **Reward at the Presence of Trigger:** When the trigger appears at the threshold distance, immediately offer the dog the reward or treat. This creates a positive association between the trigger and the reward.
- **Gradually Decrease Distance:** Over time, as the dog becomes more comfortable with the trigger's presence, gradually decrease the distance between

the dog and the trigger. The goal is to bring the dog closer to the trigger while maintaining a positive emotional response.

- **Consistency and Repetition:** Consistency is crucial in counter conditioning. Repeat the process regularly, rewarding the dog each time they encounter the trigger, to reinforce the positive association.
- **Stay Below Threshold:** If at any point the dog shows signs of discomfort or negative behavior, increase the distance to bring them back below the threshold where they feel comfortable.

Counter conditioning is a gradual process that requires patience and understanding. It helps dogs learn to associate previously feared or triggering stimuli with positive experiences, leading to a more relaxed and well-adjusted response. It's important to work at the dog's pace and avoid pushing them beyond their comfort zone. If you are unsure how to implement counter conditioning for your dog's specific issues, consulting a professional dog trainer or behaviorist can provide valuable guidance and support.

Avoid Punishment

Never punish your dog for displaying anxious behavior as it can worsen the anxiety and lead to other behavioral problems.

Medication or Supplements

In severe cases, your veterinarian may recommend medication or supplements to help reduce your dog's anxiety. This should be done under professional supervision.

Stay Calm and Patient

Be patient and understanding throughout the process. It may take time for your dog to overcome separation anxiety, but consistent and positive reinforcement will help them improve over time. Remember that every dog is unique, and the severity of separation anxiety can vary. Be flexible in your approach and be prepared to adjust the strategies based on your dog's response. If you are struggling to manage your dog's separation anxiety, don't hesitate to seek guidance from a veterinarian or a certified dog behaviorist to create a tailored plan for your furry companion.

Chapter 4
Common Mistakes to Avoid

Dog training is a vital process that strengthens the bond between you and your canine companion while promoting good behavior and a harmonious household. However, dog training can be challenging, and even with the best intentions, it's easy to make common mistakes that hinder progress that could lead to undesired behaviors. Understanding these mistakes is crucial to ensure effective and you both have positive training experiences.

Let's take a look at two common mistakes to avoid when dealing with barking issues. Ultimately, we want to foster trust and a lifelong partnership with our four-legged friends. By steering clear of these pitfalls, you can seek to bring out the best in your furry companion and strengthen the human-dog bond between you.

Mistake 1: Using Punishment and Negative Reinforcement

Negative reinforcement and punishment involves applying aversive stimuli to reduce or eliminate unwanted behaviors in dogs. However, these approaches to stop dog barking can be problematic. Here's how punishment may lead to unintended consequences and potential harm to the dog-human relationship.

Using Excessive Force: Applying negative reinforcement or punishment with excessive force can lead to physical and emotional harm to the dog. Physical punishments, such as hitting or aggressive leash corrections, can cause fear, anxiety, and even aggressive behavior in the dog.

Failing to Address the Underlying Cause: Negative reinforcement and punishment address the symptoms of unwanted behavior but may not address the underlying cause. If the root cause of the behavior, such as fear or anxiety, is not addressed, the dog may continue to exhibit problematic behaviors or develop new ones.

Creating a Negative Association with Training: If training is solely based on negative reinforcement or punishment, the dog may develop a negative association with training sessions or the trainer, making future training efforts more challenging.

Lack of Positive Reinforcement: Relying solely on negative reinforcement or punishment without incorporating positive reinforcement can lead to a lack of motivation and engagement in the training process. Positive reinforcement encourages desired behaviors and strengthens the bond between the dog and the owner.

Using Punishment for Natural Behaviors: Sometimes barking is a normal and natural response. Punishing a dog for natural behaviors, such as barking to communicate or growling as a warning, can suppress their ability to communicate effectively. This can lead to increased anxiety and confusion for the dog.

Negative Emotional Impact: The use of negative reinforcement and punishment can create fear and anxiety in dogs. This can result in a breakdown of trust between the dog and the owner, leading to behavioral issues and a compromised relationship.

Not Considering Individual Differences: Dogs have different temperaments and sensitivities. What may be considered mild punishment for one dog can be distressing or overwhelming for another. Owners must be aware of their dog's unique needs and responses.

Ignoring Positive Alternatives: There are numerous positive training methods and behavior modification techniques that are effective in shaping desired behaviors without the use of aversive stimuli. Ignoring these alternatives in favor of punishment-based methods can hinder the dog's learning experience and overall well-being.

Negative reinforcement and punishment can be counterproductive and potentially harmful. Dog owners should prioritize positive reinforcement-based training methods, as they promote a trusting and respectful relationship with their canine companions and foster a more positive and effective training experience. Consulting with a professional dog trainer who uses science-based, force-free training methods can provide valuable guidance and ensure the training process is safe and humane.

Mistake 2: Not Seeking Professional Help if Needed

In some instances it may be best to seek the help of a qualified dog trainer. Finding a reputable and qualified dog trainer to help with dog barking requires some research and consideration.

Here are some steps to help you find a suitable dog trainer:

Ask for Recommendations: Seek recommendations from friends, family, neighbors, or your veterinarian. Personal referrals can provide valuable insights into the effectiveness and professionalism of a dog trainer.

Online Search: Use search engines or online directories to find dog trainers in your local area. Look for trainers who specialize in behavior modification and have experience in dealing with barking issues.

Check Certifications and Qualifications:

Look for trainers who are certified by reputable organizations such as the Certification Council for Professional Dog Trainers (CCPDT) or the International Association of Canine Professionals (IACP). Certification indicates a commitment to professional standards and ethical training practices.

Verify the trainer's education and credentials, ensuring they have relevant experience and knowledge in behavior modification and dog training.

Read Reviews and Testimonials: Check online reviews and testimonials from previous clients to get an idea of the trainer's success rate and the experiences of other dog owners with similar issues.

Visit Training Facilities: If possible, visit the training facility and observe a training session or class. This will give you a sense of the trainer's methods, the atmosphere, and how they interact with dogs and owners.

Ask About Training Methods

Inquire about the trainer's approach to behavior modification and how they address barking issues. Look for trainers who use positive reinforcement-based methods rather than punishment-based techniques. Avoid trainers who use harsh methods, such as shock collars or physical punishment, as these can be harmful and counterproductive.

Interview the Trainer

Schedule a consultation or interview with the trainer to discuss your dog's barking problem and your training goals. Ask about their experience, training philosophy, and what kind of results you can expect.

It's essential to choose a training technique that aligns with your dog's personality, your training goals, and your personal preferences. Positive reinforcement-based methods are generally considered the most effective and humane, promoting a positive and trust-based relationship between dogs and their owners.

A good trainer should be patient, understanding, and willing to tailor the training program to meet your dog's specific needs.

There are several popular types of dog training techniques used for behavior modification. Different trainers and dog owners may prefer one or a combination of these techniques based on their training philosophy, the dog's personality, and the specific behavior being addressed. Although we've touched on some popular types of dog training techniques in the previous pages, here is a complete list of techniques trainers may use:

- **Positive Reinforcement:** Positive reinforcement training focuses on rewarding desired behaviors with treats, praise, or toys. This technique encourages dogs to repeat those behaviors to receive more rewards. It helps build a strong bond between the dog and the trainer and fosters a positive learning experience.
- **Clicker Training:** Clicker training is a form of positive reinforcement where a handheld clicker is used to mark the exact moment when the dog performs a desired behavior. The click is immediately followed by a reward, helping the dog associate the sound with positive reinforcement.
- **Operant Conditioning:** Operant conditioning involves shaping behavior through positive and negative consequences. Desirable behaviors are reinforced, while undesirable behaviors are ignored or discouraged using methods like time-outs or withholding rewards.
- **Counter Conditioning:** Counter conditioning is used to change a dog's emotional response to a specific trigger. It involves creating positive associations with previously feared or anxiety-

inducing stimuli, helping the dog become more comfortable with the trigger.

- **Desensitization:** Desensitization aims to reduce a dog's sensitivity to a particular stimulus by gradually exposing them to it at a low intensity and gradually increasing the intensity over time. It is commonly used for fear and anxiety-related behaviors.
- **Behavioral Adjustment Training (BAT):** BAT is a technique that allows dogs to make choices and learn to control their own behavior. It involves controlled exposure to triggers at a safe distance, giving the dog the option to retreat and rewarding calm behavior.
- **Constructional Aggression Treatment (CAT):** CAT is a method used to modify aggressive behavior. It involves rewarding the absence of aggression in situations that usually trigger aggressive responses.
- **Model-Rival Training:** Model-rival training involves using another dog (the "model") to demonstrate the desired behavior. The dog being trained observes the model's behavior and learns by imitation.

Check for Insurance and Bonding

Ensure that the dog trainer has liability insurance in case of any accidents or injuries during training sessions.

Ask for References

Request references from the trainer, and follow up with those references to get feedback from previous clients about their experiences.

Consider Group Classes vs. Private Sessions

Decide whether group classes or private training sessions would be more suitable for your dog's barking issues. Some dogs may benefit from the socialization opportunities in group classes, while others might require more focused attention in private sessions.

Remember that the relationship between a dog owner and a trainer is essential for successful training outcomes. Choose a trainer who communicates well, listens to your concerns, and demonstrates a genuine interest in helping you and your dog. Avoid trainers who make unrealistic promises or guarantee immediate results. Behavior modification takes time, patience, and consistent effort, so be prepared to work with the trainer in a positive and proactive manner to address your dog's barking issues.

Should You Consult a Veterinarian?

Consulting a veterinarian may be necessary if your dog barks excessively, especially if the excessive barking is a new or sudden behavior. Excessive barking can be an indicator of an underlying medical issue or behavioral problem. Here are some situations when it may be necessary to seek veterinary advice:

Sudden Change in Barking Behavior: If your dog suddenly starts barking a lot when they previously did not, it could be a sign of a medical issue, pain, or discomfort. Sudden behavior changes should always be investigated by a veterinarian.

Accompanied by Other Symptoms: If the excessive barking is accompanied by other concerning symptoms such as lethargy, loss of appetite, vomiting, diarrhea, or changes in behavior, it could indicate an underlying health problem that needs immediate attention.

Signs of Pain or Discomfort: Dogs may bark excessively if they are experiencing pain or discomfort due to injuries, dental issues, or other health problems. A veterinarian can perform a thorough examination to identify and address the source of the pain.

Behavioral Issues: Excessive barking can also be a behavioral problem, such as separation anxiety, fear, or territorial behavior. A veterinarian can help determine if the barking is due to behavioral issues and recommend appropriate training or behavioral modification techniques.

Rule Out Medical Causes: Excessive barking can sometimes be caused by medical conditions like thyroid disorders, cognitive dysfunction, or neurological issues. A veterinarian can perform diagnostic tests to rule out any medical causes.

Medication or Supplements: In some cases, a veterinarian may prescribe medications or supplements to help calm an anxious or excessively barking dog. It's important to consult a vet before giving any medication or supplement to your dog.

General Health Checkup: If your dog's excessive barking does not seem to have an obvious cause, a routine checkup with a veterinarian is still recommended to ensure they are in good health.

Professional Advice: A veterinarian can provide professional advice on managing excessive barking through behavioral training, environmental enrichment, and other techniques that promote your dog's well-being.

Remember that excessive barking can be caused by a variety of factors, and it's crucial to determine the underlying cause to address the issue effectively. A veterinarian can play a vital role in diagnosing and treating any medical issues and providing guidance on behavioral modifications to help reduce excessive barking and improve your dog's quality of life.

Conclusion

Understanding why dogs bark and employing effective methods to curb excessive barking are essential for maintaining a happy and harmonious relationship between you and your dog. Barking is a natural form of communication for dogs, serving various purposes, including expressing emotions, alerting to potential threats, and seeking attention. However, excessive barking can become problematic, leading to disruptions and distress for both the dog and the surrounding environment. By identifying the root causes of the barking, such as boredom, anxiety, or territorial behavior, dog owners can implement a combination of positive reinforcement, proper socialization, mental stimulation, and environmental management to effectively address the behavior.

Remember, it's crucial to avoid punitive methods and prioritize positive training techniques that build trust and understanding between the dog and their owner. With patience, consistency, and empathy, you can guide your canine companion towards appropriate barking behavior. Keep in mind your ultimate goal is to foster a well-mannered and content dog while strengthening the unique bond that exists between you and your beloved pet.

References

Barking: The Sound of a Language, by Turid Rugaas

How to Be Your Dog's Best Friend: The Classic Training Manual for Dog Owners, by The Monks of New Skete

How to Speak Dog: Mastering the Art of Dog-Human Communication, by Stanley Coren

Decoding Your Dog: Explaining Common Dog Behaviors and How to Prevent or Change Unwanted Ones, by American College of Veterinary Behaviorists

About the Author

Sandra Shillington began her career as a corporate writer and graphic designer. Her love of Goldendoodles and life with her dogs led her to write and illustrate the series of books, *Kai + Byrdie the Goldendoodles*. In addition, she writes how-to articles for life with Goldendoodles on her blog at KaiandByrdie.com.

Say Hi to Kai and Byrdie!

www.KaiandByrdie.com

Instagram: @KaiandByrdie
YouTube: @OurDoodleLife
TikTok: @our.doodle.life
Facebook: @KaiTheGoldendoodle

Also available on Amazon

Kai + Byrdie's storybook and coloring book!

Made in United States
North Haven, CT
08 August 2023